John Procter

The Rosary Confraternity

John Procter

The Rosary Confraternity

ISBN/EAN: 9783741138768

Manufactured in Europe, USA, Canada, Australia, Japa

Cover: Foto ©Thomas Meinert / pixelio.de

Manufactured and distributed by brebook publishing software
(www.brebook.com)

John Procter

The Rosary Confraternity

INDEX.

The Rosary Confraternity.

THE DEVOTION OF THE ROSARY.

AMONGST the most encouraging signs of the times, giving us promise of a coming harvest of souls, is the revival of devotion to the Mother of God. One of the evidences of this revival is the increased and daily increasing practice of saying the Rosary — a practice which is being taken up, with our other Catholic observances, even by many who are not of the fold. It is well that it is so. *Per Mariam ad Jesum* —Mary leads us to Jesus :

> " How can I rightly love thy Son
> Sweet Mother, if I love not thee?"

The spread of this devotion amongst Catholics is easily accounted for; it is attributable, in part at least, to the untiring zeal of our Holy Father Leo XIII., who has not ceased year by year, for some time past, to exhort the faithful to cultivate in an especial way this form of prayer to the Divine Son through the Mother.

Before speaking directly of the Rosary Confraternity it may be well to say a few words by way of preface about the Rosary as a devotion.

1.— *What is the Rosary?*

Every Catholic knows that it is a form of supplication which unites in itself mental and vocal prayer. It consists of fifteen meditations on the principal events of our Lord's life and the life of His holy Mother.

The fifteen meditations are divided into three equal parts. The first part brings before the mind the chief mysteries which gave joy to the world, viz., the Annunciation, the Visitation, the Birth of our Lord, His being offered in the Temple as a child, and His being found there as a boy of twelve : these are called the *Joyful Mysteries.* The second part of the Rosary is called the *Sorrowful Mysteries* or Decades, because it introduces to our pious notice the sorrows of our Lord's life which culminated in His sacred and saving death : the Agony and prayer in the garden, His being scourged at the pillar, His thorn-crowning, His carrying the Cross from the place of judgment to Cal-vary, and finally His Death upon the Cross for the redemption of men. In the third division of the Rosary we are led to the contemplation of His triumph, and hence it is called by the name of the *Glorious Mysteries :* these mysteries comprise His glorious Resurrection from the dead, His triumphant Ascension from earth to heaven, the coming down of the Holy Spirit upon the infant Church on Pentecost Day, the Assumption of our Lady into the -kingdom of her Son, and then her solemn coronation as Queen of earth and Queen of heaven.

The Rosary has been called "an epitome of the Gospel," recalling to us as it does the Incarnation of Jesus Christ, the consoling doctrine of the Redemption by the sacred Blood-shedding, and the hopeful and helpful teaching of the future rewards. "This is life eternal, to know Thee, the one true and living God, and Him whom Thou hast sent, Jesus Christ.* St. Paul gives us a commentary upon these words of the Divine Master: "For he that cometh to God, must

* John xvii. 3.

believe that He is, and is a rewarder of them that seek Him." * The Mysteries of the Rosary remind us that He is—that He is our Saviour and our Redeemer, and that He is our Rewarder—that He came into the world " for us men and for our salvation," that He left the world because " it was expedient for us that He should go," and that He has gone " to prepare a place " for us, so that His word may be realized : " Where I am, there shall my minister be." † This is the doctrinal part of the rosary ; these are the subjects proposed for our meditation, thus supplying spiritual food for the mind, lifting up the intellect to God, keeping alive and strengthening the theological virtues of faith, hope and love.

The Rosary Mysteries, like fifteen faithful mirrors, reflect back to us

* Heb. xi. 6.   † John xii. 26.

the ways and life, the words and actions, the joys, the sorrows and the triumphs of our Lord. As fifteen life-like pictures, they reveal to us, as in a cinematograph, the scenes and incidents of which the Gospel is the faithful record, and the historic personages who took part in them. We see Mary and Joseph and Elizabeth, and the two Johns, and Anna, and Simeon, and the Doctors of the law, Pilate and Herod, the Jews and the Roman soldiers and the Centurion, the Apostles, and the Angels on earth and in heaven ; but above them all—like Saul " head and shoulders above the prophets" —we see Jesus, the central figure around which all revolve, the Sun which illumines all, the Sheaf before which all fall down in lowly adoring love. As an eloquent preacher, eloquent beyond the power of

words, the Rosary preaches to us
"the Way, the Truth and the Life."
As a most convincing teacher it
impresses upon us, in a manner
which we cannot gainsay, "the
wonderful ways of God."

Such is the devotion as a
mental prayer or meditation, con-
secrating the mind at once and the
heart. But the lips had to be
dedicated to God as well as the
intellect and the will, and hence, as
Leo XIII. expresses it, St. Dominic
"combined, and as it were inter-
laced the subjects to be meditated
with the Angelical salutation and
with the prayer to God and the
Father of our Lord Jesus Christ." *
Whilst we meditate upon the sub-
lime truths, and while our hearts
are made to "leap up to God," to
use St. Augustine's expressive word,

* Encyclical Letter on the Rosary,
September, 1883.

"and in our meditation a fire—the fire of Divine love—breaks out,"* we unite the voice to the mind and heart, vocal prayer to mental prayer, saying, as we think of each mystery, one " Our Father," ten " Hail Marys " and one " Glory be to the Father," thus fulfilling our Lord's injunction : " When you pray, pray thus : Our Father," etc.† —thus again re-echoing the Angel's word to Mary : " Hail full of grace," etc.; ‡ thus once more vieing with the Angels in holy rivalry, and singing with them honour and praise and glory to the Blessed Three : Father, Son, and Holy Ghost.

And lest our minds should wander from our subject, lest we should be distracted by the counting of the prescribed prayers, we hold

* Ps. xxxviii. 4.   † Matt. vi. 9.
‡ Luke i. 28

the bead-string in our hands and pass a bead through our fingers for each *Pater*, *Ave* and *Gloria* that we say, so that we may know when our holy task is done. We sanctify the mind by sacred thoughts, the heart by acts of sorrow and love, the lips by the inspired words of sacred prayer, and the fingers by contact with the blessed beads. With reason then does the Sovereign Pontiff exclaim in the Encyclical already quoted : " Let the Christian people cling more and more to the practice of the Rosary, to which our ancestors had recourse as to an ever ready refuge in their distress, and as a glorious pledge of Christian faith and devotion."

***

2.—*Origin of the Rosary.*

As the Venerable Pontiff reminds us, " our ancestors in the faith, had recourse to this devotion for the past seven centuries. In the Rosary was their help, their their stay, refuge " through good report and evil report," in storm and in sunshine, in the days of the Church's sorrow and in the days of her gladness, for nearly seven hundred years. It is a tradition, which is probably beyond doubt, that St. Dominic was "the first to institute this devotion under the name of the Holy Rosary."* The precise date of the vision which the Mother of God is said to have vouchsafed to him when she made known to him this form of prayer and bade him preach it "as a devotion most pleasing to her Divine Son and to herself," is not known. Probably it was when he was preaching against the Albigenses (A.D. 1206-1216),

* Leo XIII., Encyclical, September 1883.

for then assuredly he needed a weapon with which to destroy the foxes which were threatening destruction to the vineyard of Christ, a spiritual sword with which to smite the enemies of God and men.

1. We do not claim for St. Dominic that he originated the practice of using counting beads in saying prayers. Long before his day the custom prevailed. St. Paul the Abbot of Lydia, who lived in the fifth century, repeated the *Pater* a hundred times each day and made use of little stones with which to count them. St. Benedict had "round balls fastened together by a thread" for the same purpose. St. Gertrude died in 1263, and her bead-string, consisting of little balls strung together by thin twine, was buried with her. In England also the practice prevailed. In 1040 Coun-

tess Godiva of Coventry had "a chain of pearls and precious stones whereon she was accustomed to count her prayers." An English Council in the ninth century directed that "seven belts of *Pater Nosters*" should be said for a person deceased. Paternoster-Row in London is supposed to take its name from the fact that beads for counting *Paters* were sold there. So that in using beads St. Dominic took up and propagated a pious custom, which he found but did not initiate.

2. It is needless to say that the "Founder and Inventor of the Rosary," as Pope Leo XIII. styles him, did not preach for the first time the mysteries which form the meditations of the Rosary. No, they are old as Christianity itself. Our Lord preached them, His prophets foretold them, and they have ever been the Creed of

Christendom and the comfort of the people of God.

3. How then did St. Dominic institute the Rosary? Under the inspiration of the Mother of the Divine Word he united the double prayer—the prayer of the mind and the prayer of the lips; he wedded together truth and prayer, he preached faith and practice, he lifted up the mind and heart and lips and hands of men to the God who formed the body and created the spirit or soul which made it a living temple sanctified by the indwelling of the Holy Ghost. " Truths had decayed from the minds of men ; " men were forgetting " the wondrous works of God ; " they were out of touch with the fundamental doctrines of the Incarnation, the Redemption, the Eternal Rewards ; and St. Dominic by the Rosary preached them anew.

Heresy was rampant because faith was dormant. He aroused that faith, and when faith prevailed, heresy was overcome. Error as "a cloud covered the earth," and as a mist obscured the pure light of heaven. St. Dominic by the Rosary proclaimed the truth, and the clouds were rolled back and the mists were dispersed at the rising of the Divine Sun. The Dominican Pope, St. Pius V., puts it pithily : " Christians began suddenly to be transformed into other men, the darkness of heresy to be dispelled, and the light of Catholic faith to shine forth." Then too the lips of men were sealed as though icebound, and their hearts were cold and hard as if of marble ; they did not pray, they did not speak to God. St. Dominic bade them pray as well as think, speak as well as listen, express in words the thoughts of their minds and the feelings of their hearts. Under the influence of the truths of the Incarnation and the Blood-shedding, their minds thawed, their hearts were softened, and then they who had been dumb spoke.

This was the double miracle wrought by the Rosary in St. Dominic's day. Heresy gave place to divine truth, and lips that had been sealed were opened to prayer and praise. The sign of the Son of Man was seen, "the deaf heard, the dumb spoke and to the poor the Gospel was preached." This was the double Apostolate of the Rosary originated by St. Dominic nearly seven hundred years ago—an apostolate of truth and an apostolate of prayer. This was to be the work of the Rosary to all time.

The Confraternity of the Rosary.*

When St. Dominic had received from the lips of our Lady the command to preach the devotion of the Rosary, he, as a loyal son of Holy Church, submitted the commission to the Pope of the time for his approval, sanction and blessing, knowing that to his Vicar alone our Lord had said : " Thou art Peter, and upon this rock will I build My Church ; " " Feed My lambs, feed My sheep ; " " Confirm thy brethren." Under the guidance of the Sovereign Pontiff St. Dominic formed the Rosary Confraternity— that is to say, he induced good and

* The Confraternity mu-t not be confounded with the *Living Rosary* or the *Perpetual Rosary*. which are totally distinct organizations.

faithful Catholics to show their loyalty to God and their devotion to His holy Mother by forming themselves into a sodality, the members of which undertook (though not under pain of sin) to say the Rosary fervently and devoutly at stated and regular times.

The idea of association rests upon the principle which has its equivalent in every tongue: " Union is strength." Christian association for the purpose of prayer and good works has the immediate sanction of our Lord Himself : " Where two or three are gathered together in My name, there am I in their midst." * Alone we fall, with others we stand; alone we fail, with others we succeed ; alone we are discouraged and disheartened, with others we are aroused to

* Matt. xviii. 20.

enthusiasm and courage. "A brother helped by a brother is a strong city;"* "Woe to the man who is alone;"† for "it is not good for man to be alone."‡

Evil men combine for evil purposes; why should not good men combine in holy work and united prayer? Worldly men form societies, companies and associations for the furtherance of their worldly aims; why should not the children of God unite and form societies, sodalities, confraternities to further the interests of God and the salvation of souls? Our Holy Father Leo XIII., in his Encyclical on the Rosary Confraternity published in September 1897, speaks of these associations with the greatest praise:

"The natural tendency of man

* Proverbs xviii. 19.   † Eccl. iv. 10.
‡ Gen. ii. 18.

to association has never been
stronger, or more earnestly and
generally followed, than in our own
age. This is not at all to be repre-
hended, unless when so excellent a
natural tendency is perverted to evil
purposes, and wicked men, binding
together in various forms of societies,
conspire 'against the Lord and
against His Christ' (Ps. ii. 2). It
is, however, most gratifying to
observe that pious associations are
becoming more and more popular
among Catholics also. They are
frequently formed; indeed, all
Catholics are so closely drawn
together and united by the bonds of
charity, as members of one house-
hold, that they both may be and
are truly styled brethren."

Amongst these associations or
sodalities probably the most venerable and the most richly indulgenced, as well as the most

simple and most fruitful, is that of the Holy Rosary. In the Encyclical just alluded to Leo XIII goes on to say, in words which are weighty as coming from the Vicar of Christ himself and as addressed to the Church throughout the world :

" We do not hesitate to assign a pre-eminent place among these Societies to that known as the Society of the Holy Rosary. If we regard its origin, we find it distinguished by its antiquity, for St. Dominic himself is said to have been its founder. If we estimate its privileges, we see it enriched with a vast number of them granted by the munificence of Our predecessors. The form of the association, its very soul, is the Rosary of Our Lady, of the excellency of which We have elsewhere spoken at length. Still the virtue and efficacy of the Rosary appear all the greater when considered as the special office of the sodality which bears its name.

"Every one knows how necessary prayer is for all men; not that God's decrees can be changed, but, as St. Gregory says, 'that men by asking may merit to receive what Almighty God hath decreed from eternity to grant them' (Dialog. lib. i. c. 8). And St. Augustine says, 'He who knoweth how to pray aright, knoweth how to live aright' (In Ps. cxviii) But prayers acquire their g eatest efficacy in obtaining God's assistance when offered publicly, by large numbers, constantly, and unanimously, so as to form, as it were, a single chorus of supplication; as those words of the Acts of the Apostles clearly declare, wherein the disciples of Christ, awaiting the coming of the Holy Ghost, are said to have been 'persevering with one mind in prayer.' (Acts i. 14). Those who practise this manner of prayer will never fail to obtain certain fruit.

"Such is certainly the case with members of the Rosary Sodality. Just as, by the recitation of the Divine Office, priests offer a public, constant and most efficacious supplication, so the supplication offered by the members of this sodality in the recitation of the Rosary, or 'Psalter of Our Lady,' as it has been styled by some of the Popes, is also in a way public, constant, and universal."

How to become Members of the Confraternity.

The conditions of membership are simple to a degree. They may be reduced to two.

(1) People who wish to join the Sodality must have their names entered on the Register of the Confraternity canonically erected, either in a Dominican church or by authority of the Dominican General in some other church. *

* For the establishment of the Confraternity it is necessary (1) to have a patent of erection from the General of the Dominican Order, which may be applied for through the Dominican Provincial ; (2) to have the written consent of the Ordinary of the Diocese. The erection is generally made by a Dominican Father deputed by the General. The Director of the Confraternity so erected can then enrol members, bless beads and do all that the Dominican Fathers do.

A priest who has power to bless beads and enrol members is bound under pain of nullity to send the names of those whom he receives to be entered on the Register kept in a church where the Confraternity is erected.

It may be well to make note of the following decisions of the Sacred Congregation of Indulgences :

1. The full Christian and surname should be entered, or in the case of religious the name by which they are called in Religion.

2. A priest who has the faculty to enrol associates may also put his own name on the Register.

3. Any person who is unable to go to a church where the Confraternity exists, may send his or her name by post or by some one else to the Rev. Father Director to be inscribed on the Register.

(See list of churches in the appendix.)

4. Children who have not come to the use of reason should not be received into the Confraternity ; nor should people send the names of their relatives or friends for enrolment except with their knowledge and consent.

(2) The second condition for gaining all the Indulgences is that the beads be blessed either by a Dominican Father or by a priest who has faculties from the General of the Dominican Order.*

Again it may be of help to others if we state here that :

(*a*) A Rosary is blessed *for an individual ;* consequently if it is given away it must be re-blessed for the one to whom it is given; if it is lent to another the borrower

* These may be procured through the Dominican Provincial.

does not gain the indulgences, but by lending it the lender does not lose them, so that when it is returned, it need not be blessed again : the former blessing remains.

(*b*)   If a number of Rosaries are blessed for distribution, each one is blessed for the first person who receives it and uses it.

(*c*)   If Rosaries are sold *after* they have been blessed, they lose the Indulgences *ipso facto*, even though no addition is made to the price on account of the blessing (which would be simony). Those who sell Rosary beads may, of course, get them blessed afterwards for the purchaser, but they must not be blessed and then sold. This has twice been decided by the Sacred Congregation of Indulgences.

(*d*)   If after the blessing three or four beads only are lost, there is no need to have the Rosary re-blessed ; but if a notable part of the Rosary be lost, then the blessing should be repeated. If the bead-string or wire breaks and the beads are not lost from their places, a new blessing is not required.

(*e*) It is necessary to use the prescribed form of blessing for the Confraternity ; the sign of the Cross made over the Rosary is not sufficient.

(*f*) Only Rosaries of five, ten, or fifteen decades may be blessed with the Confraternity blessing. Consequently Rosaries of six or seven decades may not be indulgenced, unless some special dispensation be granted, e.g., to members of religious orders who use six decade beads.

(*g*) When a number say the Rosary together, it is sufficient if the leader uses blessed beads ; the

others need not do so. In some
convents and in Béguinages the
Rosary is said publicly whilst the
sisters work ; in these cases only
one need use blessed beads, i.e.,
the one who leads or presides at the
recitation.

(*h*) When the Pope blesses
beads, His Holiness does not
usually intend to give the Dominican or Confraternity blessing Such
beads should be again blessed
by one having the Dominican
faculty.

(*i*) When the Confraternity
blessing is given to Rosaries which
are already blessed either by the
Pope or by some one having
special powers, the former blessing
is not affected by the Confraternity
blessing. which only adds to the
existing Indulgences.

(*k*) Rosary rings may not be
indulgenced, no matter of what

material they may be made.

N.B.—Beads may be sent by post to be blessed to a Dominican church or to any priest who holds the special faculties ; but *stamps for the return postage* and the *address clearly. and distinctly written* should always accompany them. They should be addressed to " The Rev. Father Director of the Rosary Confraternity."

OBLIGATIONS OF MEMBERS.

The only obligations which members take upon themselves are :

1. To say the 15 decades each week.

2. To meditate upon the subject of each mystery as the prescribed prayers are said.

N.B.—(1) These obligations are in no way binding under pain of sin ; but if the entire Rosary is not said during the week, the member will forfeit many of the Indulgences.

(2) Religious and others who by Rule or pious custom say the Rosary every day, satisfy the obligations of the Confraternity by this recital, and need not say an additional Rosary.

(3) It is not necessary for the Confraternity obligation to say the fifteen decades at the same time or even on the same day. Five mysteries or even one mystery, may be said at a time. Provided the whole Rosary is said during the week, the mysteries may be divided at pleasure for some of the Indulgences, though for the gaining of others five decades should be said at a time.

———

Advantages of the Confraternity.

1.—*Union of Prayer.*

The first advantage of the Confraternity is the one to which we have alluded, united prayer. As members of the Confraternity we are not alone, we are united to the members who have existed during the past seven hundred years—to members on earth, in heaven and in the suffering state. We are one with the thousands and tens of thousands banded together throughout the world—in England, Ireland, Scotland, Wales, in Italy, Spain, France, Austria, in the vast continents of Australia, America, New Zealand, Africa, in a word in every land where the Gospel has been preached and the Cross of Christ has been planted. What a wondrous power is this great chorus of prayer, and prayer ascending hourly by day and by night, nay, every minute of the day and the night to the celestial throne! And yet each member has a share in the merits and prayers of the others. Our Holy Father, Leo XIII., sums up in his Encyclical of September 1897 all that we would say :

" Since, as We have said, public prayers are much more excellent and more efficacious than private ones, so ecclesiastical writers have given to the Rosary Sodality the title of ' the army of prayer, enrolled by St. Dominic under the banner of the Mother of God '—of her whom sacred literature and the history of the Church salute as the conqueror of the Evil One and of all errors. The Rosary unites together all who join the Sodality in a common bond of paternal or military comradeship ; so that a

mighty host is thereby formed, duly
marshalled and arrayed, to repel the
assaults of the enemy both from
within and without. Wherefore
may the members of this pious
society take to themselves the
words of St. Cyprian : 'Our prayer
is public and in common ; and
when we pray, we pray not for one,
but for the whole people, for we,
the entire people, are one' (De
Orat. Domin.) The history of the
Church bears testimony to the
power and efficacy of this form of
prayer, recording as it does the
rout of the Turkish forces at the
naval battle of Lepanto, and the
victories gained over the same in the
last century at Temesvar in Hungary
and in the island of Corfu. Our
predecessor, Gregory XIII., in order
to perpetuate the memory of the
first-named victory, established the
Feast of Our Lady of Victories,

which later on Clement **XI.** distinguished by the title of Rosary Sunday, and commanded it to be celebrated throughout the universal Church."

2.—*Suffrages for the Dead.*

We have a duty to others as well as to ourselves, a duty not only to the living but to the dead. In saying the Rosary we can help the one and give comfort to the other. "When the dead is at rest, let his remembrance remain, and comfort him in the departure of his spirit."* How better remember the dead, how more effectually comfort the departed spirit, than by gaining Indulgences for him? And to what devotion have more Indulgences been granted than to the Rosary, "the Queen of Indulgenced Prayers"? It is consoling to re-

* Ecclus xxxviii. 24.

member that all these spiritual
treasures to which we shall presently
refer are applicable by way of
suffrage to the suffering dead,
whether in life they belonged to the
Confraternity or not. In some
places it is customary when offering
the Rosary for the faithful dead to
say at the end of each decade
instead of the " Glory be to the
Father " the invocation, " Eternal
rest give unto them, O Lord," &c.
There is no reason why this should
not be done ; indeed it is a practice
which might with spiritual profit be
universally introduced.

3.—*Indulgences of the Rosary Confraternity.*

The Indulgences of the Rosary,
being very many and very great,
naturally constitute one of the
advantages of membership of the
Confraternity, for although some of

them may be gained by non-members, only those who have been enrolled in the Confraternity can gain all. Before giving the list of some of these spiritual graces granted by the Church, it is well to bear in mind that the devotion and the Confraternity have existed for nearly seven centuries and that many Pontiffs have added to the number. It is on record that Pius IX., one day speaking of the innumerable treasures in the Palace of the Popes, took his Rosary in his hand and said, " Behold the greatest treasure of the Vatican !" The Rosary is the greatest treasure of the Vatican because the Vatican has made it so, as the following authentic *List of Indulgences* with their conditions will show:

On the Day of Admission or on the nearest festival or Sunday following.

1. PLENARY—Contrition, Confession, Communion.

2. PLENARY—Contrition, Confession, Communion, in the Church or Chapel of the Confraternity ; the recitation of a third part of the Rosary (i.e., any Five Mysteries), and prayer for the peace of the Church.

On Rosary Sunday and on the Eve of that Feast.

1. ALL THE FAITHFUL can gain the *toties quoties* Indulgence, i.e., a distinct Plenary Indulgence for each separate visit to the Rosary Chapel or Altar, on condition of (1) Confession and Communion, (2) Prayer for the Pope's Intentions. *This Indulgence is equivalent to the Portiuncula Indulgence.*

2. All the Indulgences of the 1st Sunday of the month.

3. PLENARY—On the same conditions, to all the faithful on any one day within the octave ; Confession, Communion.

For performing the October Devotions.

1. PLENARY—To all the faithful who assist at the Rosary devotions ten times (or who perform them ten times privately, when impeded) ; Confession, Communion (Leo XIII., 1885).

2. PLENARY—To all who assist at the

devotions during the whole month ; Contrition, Confession, Communion ; prayers for the Pope's Intentions. (Pius IX., 1868.)

On the Feasts of the Mysteries of the Rosary.

1. PLENARY—Contrition, Confession, Communion ; visit to the Chapel of the Rosary.

These feasts are : Annunciation, March 25 ; Visitation, July 2 ; Nativity, December 25 ; Presentation, February 2 ; Crucifixion, Friday after Passion Sunday ; Resurrection, Easter Sunday ; Ascension, Feast ; Descent of the Holy Ghost, Whit Sunday ; Assumption, August 15 ; Coronation, November 1.

On Feasts of Our Lady.

1. PLENARY—Contrition ; visit to the Chapel of the Rosary.

These feasts are—The Immaculate Conception, Nativity, Presentation, Annunciation, Purification, Visitation, and Assumption.

(a) This Indulgence can be gained by fulfilling the same conditions on any day within the octave of the above feasts.

(b) The same Indulgence can be gained on the above days by Confession, Communion ; visit to any church or public oratory, with prayers for the Pope's Intentions.

2. PLENARY — Confession, Communion ; visit to Rosary chapel ; prayers for the Pope's Intentions on all the above

feasts, except the Presentation and Visitation.

3. PLENARY — Contrition ; assistance at the Rosary Procession on the feasts mentioned in No. 1.

4. PLENARY—On the Annunciation :— Contrition, Confession, Communion ; the Rosary.

5. PLENARY—On the Assumption :— Contrition, Confession, Communion ; visit to the Church of the Confraternity ; prayers for the Pope's Intentions.

On the Feasts of Dominican Saints.

1. PLENARY—To all ; Communion in a Dominican Church ; prayers for the Pope's Intentions.

2. PLENARY — On the feast of St. Dominic ; Confession, Communion ; visit to the Chapel of the Rosary ; prayers for the Pope's Intentions.

On other Days of the Year.

1. PLENARY—On Easter, Ascension and Pentecost days, and on any two Fridays in Lent ; Confession, Communion ; visit to church ; prayers for the Pope's Intentions.

2. PLENARY—On Corpus Christi, the Third Sunday of April, the Sunday after the Nativity of the B. V. Mary, the feast

of the Patron Saint of the Church ; Contrition, Confession, Communion ; visit to the Altar of the Rosary ; prayers, &c.

On the First Sunday of each Month.

1. PLENARY—Contrition, Confession, Communion, in a Church where the Confraternity is erected ; prayers for the Pope's Intentions (i. e., for the extirpation of heresy, for peace among Christian princes, and for the exaltation of our holy Mother the Church).

2. PLENARY—Contrition, Confession, Communion ; visit to the Chapel of the Rosary.

3. PLENARY—Contrition, Confession, Communion ; assistance at the Procession of the Rosary ; prayers for the Pope's Intentions.

On the Last Sunday of the Month.

1. PLENARY—To all the faithful who are in the habit of reciting with other persons a third part of the Rosary, at least three times a week ; Contrition, Confession, Communion ; visit to a Church ; prayers for the Pope's Intentions.

For saying the Rosary.

1. PLENARY—Once a month ; daily recitation of Five Mysteries ; Confession,

Communion; visit to a Church; prayers, &c.

2. PLENARY—Every time one says the whole Rosary. (Clem. IX., " Exponi Nobis.")

3. 60,000 years, and as many quarantines, every time one says Five Mysteries; Confession. (Innoc. VIII., " Splendor Patris Æterni.")

Weekly Confession, when habitual, suffices for gaining all the Indulgences, Plenary and Partial. obtainable within the week.

4. 5 years and 5 quarantines, or 2,025 days, at every pronounciation of the Sacred Name of " Jesus " in the " Hail Mary " of the Rosary.*

5. 100 days for every "Our Father" and " Hail Mary " of the Rosary.

6 50 years once a day : Five Mysteries in the Church of the Confraternity.

This Indulgence can be gained in any Church or Oratory in places where the Confraternity is not erected.

For assistance at the Votive Mass of the Rosary permitted to be said in the Dominican Churches on Wednesdays and Saturdays.

I. PLENARY—Assistance; prayers for the Pope's Intentions. (Clem. X., " Cœlestium munerum.")

* See Appendix.

2. PLENARY—Once a month, to those who are in the habit of assisting at this Mass ; Contrition, Confession, Communion.

For various Pious Works.

1. 100 years and 100 quarantines, or 40,500 days once a day to those who carry the beads about them in honour of the Blessed Virgin.

2. Many Plenary Indulgences for the performance of divers works of piety, and an almost countless number of Partial ones for the recitation of the Rosary, for visits to the Rosary Altar and Churches of the Confraternity, and others, for assisting at the Votive Mass of the Rosary, for assisting at Mass, making meditation, and, in general, for " every work of charity or piety " that a member may perform.

To Sick Members and Others.

1. PLENARY—To the sick and those lawfully hindered from assisting at the Rosary Procession on the first Sunday of the month : The entire Rosary.

2. PLENARY—To the sick and those lawfully hindered from making the required visit to the Chapel of the Rosary on the feasts of the Mysteries of the Rosary : Five Mysteries.

N.B.—Confessors have power to commute the conditions of Communion, visit, &c., in favour of the infirm in all cases in which these conditions are prescribed.

This commutation should be made at the time of Confession.

To the Dying.

1. PLENARY—Confession, Communion.

2. PLENARY—To faithful members who receive the absolution of the Rosary.

3. PLENARY—To those who hold the blessed candle of the Rosary when dying.

4. PLENARY—Reception of the last Sacraments and recitation of the "Hail, Holy Queen."

5. PLENARY—To those who invoke the Sacred Name of Jesus, at least in heart, or who give any sign of sorrow ; Contrition, Confession, Communion.

For the Dead.

1. All the altars in Dominican churches are "privileged" for Dominican Priests.

N.B.—A "privileged Altar" is an altar to which is attached a Plenary Indulgence in favour of a soul in Purgatory. This Indulgence can be applied according to the intention of the Priest who celebrates.

2. The Rosary Altar in a church where the Confraternity is erected is

"privileged" in favour of all Priests who
are Members.

3.   The Rosary Altar is "privileged"
for all Priests in churches where there is
no other "privileged" Altar.

As we have already said all the Indulgences of
the Rosary are applicable to the souls in
Purgatory.

Other Privileges granted to Members.

The Members of the Confraternity share
both in life and after death in all the
Masses, prayers, and good works of the
entire Dominican Order, and of the Confraternities attached to it.

Finally, Members belonging to the Confraternity erected in a Dominican church
enjoy all the " Privileges and Indulgences
granted to all other Confraternities, of
whatsoever kind or name." (Benedict
XIII., " Pretiosus," May 26, 1727.)

From the above list, which,
though authentic, is not complete,
we see why Pope Pius IX. spoke of
the Rosary as "the greatest treasure
of the Vatican," and we understand
the meaning of Father Faber's
words when he called it "The
Queen of Indulgenced of Prayers."

CONDITIONS FOR GAINING THE INDULGENCES.

Before ending we may add a few words as to the conditions for gaining Indulgences generally and those of the Rosary Confraternity in particular. They are taken from the declarations of the Sacred Congregation of Indulgences :

1. The contrition mentioned as required for the gaining of an Indulgence is not an actual condition, but only a necessary disposition, and indicates merely that the recipient must be in the state of grace.

2. Weekly Confession, when habitual, suffices for gaining all the Indulgences, Plenary and Partial, obtainable within the week.

3. One Communion suffices to gain many Plenary Indulgences.

4. Communion on Saturday, or on the Vigil of a feast, suffices, provided the other conditions prescribed be performed on the Sunday or feast following.

5. Those unable to receive Holy Communion at the hour of death can gain the Plenary Indulgence in which the condition of Communion is required, by invoking the Sacred Name of " Jesus," at least in heart when they cannot do so by word.

6. The visit to the church, &c., can be made either before or after Communion.

7. The Prayers offered in the Indulgenced Church at the time of Mass or Communion suffice for the visit.

8. The chapels of Convents, Workhouses, Seminaries, etc., may be looked on as public Oratories in favour of those living in them.

9. Members who cannot visit the church of the Confraternity, can fulfil the condition by visiting their Parish or Conventual church.

10. The Rosary or other prayers prescribed for gaining the above Indulgences need not be said kneeling.

11. The Indulgences of the Rosary are not suspended during the solemn year of the Jubilee, unless special mention of this fact be made in the Papal Bull proclaiming the Jubilee Indulgence.

CONCLUSION.

We will end with the words of the venerable and zealous Apostle of the Rosary in this nineteenth age. Speaking to the Rulers of the Church, Pope Leo XIII. says : " For these reasons the Roman Pontiffs have ever given the highest praise to this Sodality of our Lady.

Innocent VII. called it 'a most
devout Confraternity.' Pius V. de-
clares that by its virtue 'Christians
began suddenly to be transformed
into other men, the darkness of
heresy to be dispelled, and the light
of Catholic faith to shine forth.'
We also, Venerable Brethren,
moved by the example of Our
predecessors, earnestly exhort and
conjure you, as We have often done,
to devote special care to this sacred
warfare, so that by your efforts fresh
forces may be daily enrolled on
every side. Through you and those
of your clergy who have the care of
souls, let the people know and duly
appreciate the efficacy of this
Sodality and its usefulness for man's
salvation." * To the faithful laity
the Pontiff's fatherly words are no
less strong : " For this reason do
We exhort all Christians to give

* Encyclical, Sept. 1897.

themselves to the daily recital of this pious devotion either in public or privately in the home or family of each. . . . We believe it to be in the designs of Providence that, in these times of trial for the Church, the ancient devotion to the august Virgin should live and flourish.

" May the Christian people, excited by Our exhortations and inflamed by your appeals, now seek the protection of Mary, with an ardour growing greater day by day. Let them betake themselves more and more to the protection of Mary, and trust in her. Let them cling more and more to the practice of the Rosary, to which our ancestors had recourse as an ever-ready refuge in misfortune, and as a glorious pledge and proof of Christian faith and devotion.

" The heavenly Patroness of the

human race will receive with joy these prayers and supplications, and will easily obtain that the good grow in goodness, and that the erring repent and be brought back to salvation ; that God, who is the avenger of crime, moved to compassion and mercy, shall deliver Christendom and civil society from their present dangers, and restore to them that peace which is so much desired.

"Encouraged by this hope, We beseech God Himself, with the earnest desire of Our heart, to grant you, Venerable Brethren, every gift of heavenly blessing, through her in whom He has placed the fulness of all grace." *

* Encyclical, September 1883.

APPENDIX I.

The following are some of the churches where the Rosary Confraternity is established, and where consequently people can be enrolled or send beads to be blessed.

IN ENGLAND.

Birmingham—The Cathedral.
Bradford—St. Cuthbert's.
Buckfastleigh, Devonshire.
Chester—St. Werburgh's.
Chudleigh, Devonshire.
Clevedon—Franciscan Church.
Clifton—The Cathedral.
Cressingham, Reading.
Elton, near Bury, Lancashire.
Glossop—St. Mary's.
Halifax—St. Bernard's.
Hanwell, near London.
Haslingden—St. Mary's.
Hinckley—St. Peter's Priory.
Jersey—St. Martin's.
   ,,   St. Matthias.
Leeds—The Cathedral.
Leicester—Holy Cross Priory.
Liverpool—St. Francis Xavier.
   ..   St. Philip's.

Liverpool—Our Lady, Eldon Place.
,,   St. Oswald's, Old Swan.
London—St. Dominic's Priory, N.W.
,,   The Oratory, S.W.
,,   Church of the Rosary, Maryle-
       bone Road.
Longridge, near Preston.
Manchester—St. Chad's.
Marychurch, Torquay.
Middlesborough —The Cathedral.
Miles Platting, Manchester.
Newcastle-on-Tyne—St. Dominic's Priory.
Northwich—St. Wilfrid's
Plymouth—The Cathedral.
Rochdale—St. John's.
Rugeley, Staffs.—Hawkesyard Priory.
Silvertown, London, E.
Stoke-on-Trent—Our Lady.
Stone, Staffs.—The Immaculate Concep-
     tion and St. Dominic.
Stretford, near Manchester.
Stroud—Church of the Immaculate Con-
     ception.
Ushaw College, Durham.
Withington, Manchester.
Wolverhampton—SS. Mary and John.
Woodchester—Dominican Priory.
Woodford Green, Essex S.—Francis.

IN IRELAND.

Drogheda—St. Mary Magdalen.
Dublin—St. Saviour's.
Dundalk—St. Malachy's
Galway—Our Lady of the Assumption.
Kilkenny—Holy Trinity Church.
Limerick—St. Saviour's.
Newbridge—St. Eustace.
Newry—Sacred Heart and St. Catherine.
Portumna—SS. Peter and Paul.
Sligo—Holy Cross.
Tralee—Holy Cross.
Tallaght—Our Lady of the Rosary.
Waterford—St. Saviour's.

APPENDIX II.

THE INDULGENCE OF 2025 DAYS.

The Indulgence of 2025 days, which may be gained by members of the Confraternity for each *Ave* said as part of the Rosary, is by no means the largest of the Indulgences granted to this "Queen of Indulgenced Prayers;" but we single it out from the rest—richer though many of them are in spiritual graces —because its authenticity has been

called in question. We hope by
giving the history of its concession
that we may be able to reassure
members of the Confraternity, and
to convince them that there is no
reason whatever to doubt its being
genuine and authentic, and to remind them that in saying their
Rosary, besides gaining very many
and very great Indulgences, they
are carrying out the work of the
Apostleship of the Holy Name.

To understand the reason why
this Indulgence was granted, it is
necessary to premise that before the
eleventh or twelfth century the
custom prevailed, certainly in the
Church's liturgy, and probably
amongst the Church's children even
in their private devotions, of ending
the *Ave* or " Hail Mary " with
the words, " Blessed is the fruit of
thy womb," without the addition
which is made now of the Holy
Name Jesus. It was not till the

sixteenth century that the second part of the *Ave*—the prayer of petition, "Holy Mary, Mother of God," etc.—was added in common use to the angelical salutation, at all events in the liturgical services. Even to this day in the Office of Our Lady according to the Dominican Rite, which was composed several centuries ago, the *Ave* is said at the beginning of all the Hours, but only the first part, *i.e.*, the Angelical Salutation, without the prayer of invocation, which is, as we have said, of comparatively recent date. In the thirteenth century— to give the precise date, in 1261— the Pope (Urban IV.), to promote devotion to the Holy Name, ordered that it should be added to the *Ave*, thus : " Blessed is the fruit of thy womb, Jesus," and to encourage the faithful to conform to this rule, he granted an Indulgence to all who should do so.   In the year 1372,

Pope John **XXII.** renewed the wish
of Pope Urban, and confirmed the
Indulgence granted by him.

Now we come to the *Rosary
Indulgence.* In order still further
to encourage this pious practice in-
stituted by his predecessors (Urban
IV. and John XXII.), Innocent
VIII. granted the Indulgence tu
which we are referring, not to all
the faithful, but to all members of
the Rosary Confraternity, provided
that they devoutly added the sacred
Name of Jesus to the scriptural
words of S. Elizabeth : " Blessed is
the fruit of thy womb." The concession occurs in a Bull which begins
Splendor æternæ gloriæ, and which
was promulgated by the Sovereign
Pontiff on February 26, 1491. After
granting certain other Indulgences
to the members—such as 60,000
years and as many *quadragenas* to
all Rosarians who having been to
confession, and being repentant,

shall say a third part (i.e. five decades) of the Rosary; and 100 years and as many *quadragenas* to all who being repentant shall carry a Rosary about with them—the Bull goes on to say : " And also if the aforesaid members of the Confraternity shall pronounce the Name of *Jesus* at the end of each Angelical Salutation, We grant them for all future time five years and as many *quadragenas.*" A year represents 365 days, and a *quadragena* 40 days, so that put into modern language this Indulgence means 2025 days—thus :

Five years are equivalent to 1825 days.
Five *quadragenas* represent 200 days.
———
Total ... 2025 days.

The Pope gives his reason for granting this Indulgence in these words : " We, therefore. desiring that the brethren and sisters shall assiduously cultivate a greater devotion to the Rosary, on account of the reverence due to Mary the Virgin, and that they shall repeat the Holy Name of Jesus at the end of the Angelical Salutation, that thus they may be refreshed with a greater gift of heavenly grace, grant," etc.

Such is the Indulgence, and such the motive that prompted its concession from the sacred treasury of the Church. It was granted "for all future times," and it has never been explicitly or implicitly withdrawn. Quite the reverse, it has repeatedly been confirmed. The Bull of Innocent VIII., *Splendor æternæ gloriæ,* with all its clauses, is reproduced in "Acta Sanctæ Sedis . . . . pro Societate SS. Rosarii " published as late as 1890. The Indulgence is found in all the authorised lists of Indulgences, notably in the *Summary of Indulgences,* published by the authority of Innocent XI. on July 31, 1679, and in the *Summary* issued by the authority of Pius IX. on September 18, 1862. It also occurs in the Latin list of Indulgences which at the present day is sent from Rome to the churches in which the Confraternity is established, and which bears the seal of the Dominican General and the signature of *F. Cardinal Asquinius Praef.*, and in which it is stated that "at an audience with His Holiness on September 18, 1862, Pius IX. confirmed each and all the Indulgences contained in this summary."

To put the matter beyond all doubt, and to solve a difficulty which had arisen, on April 14, 1866, the Sacred Congregation of Indulgences was asked whether this Indulgence could be gained at the end of each *Ave*, or only at the end of each *Decade* of the Rosary? Here is the answer : "His Holiness graciously granted for ever that this

Indulgence (i.e. the 2025 days) may be gained by the members for each invocation of the Holy Name of Jesus at the end of the Angelic Salutation."

Surely, then, "Rome has spoken" with no uncertain voice; and Rome having spoken, surely "the question is settled."

Members of the Rosary Confraternity—i.e., those who at any time have been received into the Rosary Confraternity, properly so called, (*not the Living Rosary*, which is a distinct organization), by a Dominican Father, or other priest having faculties for the purpose from the Dominican Order—may, then, rest assured that in saying the Rosary devoutly, and reverently pronouncing the Holy Name at the end of the *Ave*, they can for each and for every such invocation gain an Indulgence—applicable to themselves or to the souls in Purgatory—of 2025 days.

MEMORIAL OF ADMISSION
TO THE
ROSARY CONFRATERNITY.

I ....

was admitted to the Rosary Con-

fraternity by the Rev...... ....

.........................in the Church

of...... . ... on the......

day of...................18......

www.ingramcontent.com/pod-product-compliance
Lightning Source LLC
Chambersburg PA
CBHW021538270326
41930CB00008B/1302